RED
Wide Range Readers
Phyllis Flowerdew

Oliver & Boyd

Illustrated by Caroline Sharpe

OLIVER & BOYD
Longman House
Burnt Mill
Harlow
Essex CM20 2JE
An Imprint of Longman Group UK Ltd

First published 1980
Ninth impression 1991

© Phyllis Flowerdew 1980

All rights reserved; no part of this publication may be
reproduced, stored in a retrieval system, or transmitted
in any form or by any means, electronic, mechanical,
photocopying, recording, or otherwise without the prior
written permission of the Publishers or a licence permitting
restricted copying in the United Kingdom issued by the
Copyright Licensing Agency Ltd, 33-34 Alfred Place,
London, WC1E 7DP.

ISBN 0 05 003187 2

Produced by Longman Group (FE) Ltd.
Printed in Hong Kong

Preface

There are six Wide Range Readers Red Books. They can be used alone or with Wide Range Readers Blue and Green, with which they are parallel. The controlled vocabulary and graded sentence structure make them suitable for children with the following reading ages:—

7 to 7½ years	— Book 1
7½ to 8 years	— Book 2
8 to 8½ years	— Book 3
8½ to 9 years	— Book 4
9 to 10 years	— Book 5
10 to 11+ years	— Book 6

The success of Wide Range Blue and Green Books has been proved through the years, and the author hopes that the addition of the Red series will bring pleasure to teachers and children.

Where to Find the Stories

Uncle Peppi and his Donkey   5
Small Poems   15
Ragabones Rabbit   16
Chick's Poem   26
Spider   26
The Unkind Monkey   27
A Page of Riddles   31
Treasure in the Well   32
Funny Fish   42
The Jumping Plate   43
The Blue Jackal   52
Up and Down   59
The Forest   59
A Swan for the Winter   60
Bricks and Mortar   70
The Canoe Race   72
Keys   81
How the Blackbird Became Black   82
Dog Driver   89
A Kangaroo Tale   90
Easter Egg   100
Ragabones Rabbit and Little Owl   101
Snow   110
The Christmas Tree   111
The Red Sledge   112
Small Stories   121
A Nonsense Tale   122
Helpful Teddy   128

Uncle Peppi and his Donkey

The block of flats was finished.
It rose like a tall, white tower
into the blue sky.
It had twelve floors
and ninety-six flats,
all new and clean and shining.

Along the street came the people
who were going to live in them.
Some were moving on that day,
and others were coming along
to help them.
They all knew each other,
for they all lived in the same part
of the city.

They lived in shabby little houses
with roofs that were falling in
and doors that were falling off.
But now they were going to live
in these fine, new flats.

There were mothers and fathers
and noisy children and crying babies
and barking dogs.
Some families had small vans
but others pushed their things along
on wooden hand-carts.
Some carried a chair or a table
or a rolled-up mattress.
Some carried a few pots and pans
or a baby's cradle.

Up to the door of the flats they came,
and with them came Uncle Peppi
and his grey donkey.

"What number is your flat?"
someone asked him.

"Ninety-six. It's on the top floor."

"That's nice," said someone else.
"You'll be able to see out
right across the country."

"I don't know," replied Uncle Peppi.
"I'm afraid my donkey might not like it."

"Oh, he'll soon get used to it,"
said one of the men.

"Here, take him up in the lift and see."

"A lift!" cried some of the children,
for they had never been in a lift before.

"Come along," said Uncle Peppi,
pulling gently at his donkey's collar,
but the donkey stuck out his four legs
and would not move.

"Come on. Come in the lift with me,"
said Uncle Peppi, pulling harder,
but the donkey stuck out his four legs
and would not move.

Mothers and fathers and children
tried to help.
They pulled and pushed the donkey
but no one
could get him to go into the lift.

"It's no good," said Uncle Peppi at last. "We'll have to go back home."

So Uncle Peppi and his grey donkey went back to their shabby little house with the roof falling in
and the door falling off.

Next day a little girl came to Uncle Peppi and said,

"Uncle Peppi, there are some stairs at the side of the flats.
Why don't you take your donkey up the stairs?"

"All right," said Uncle Peppi. "I will."

So Uncle Peppi and his grey donkey went along with the people
who were moving on *that* day.

"What number is your flat?" someone asked him.

"Ninety-six. It's on the top floor."

"You'll have a lot of stairs to climb."

"Yes, I shall," said Uncle Peppi.

"Come along," he said to his
donkey, pulling gently at its collar,
but the donkey stuck out his four legs
and would not move.

"Come on. Come up the stairs with me,"
said Uncle Peppi, pulling harder,
but the donkey stuck out his four legs
and would not move.

Mothers and fathers and children
tried to help.
They pulled and pushed the donkey,
but no one
could get him to go up the stairs.

"It's no good," said Uncle Peppi at
last. "We'll have to go back home."
So Uncle Peppi and his grey donkey
went back to their shabby little house
with the roof falling in
and the door falling off.

Next day a little boy came
to Uncle Peppi and said,
"Uncle Peppi, there's a crane
outside the flats. It's taking up
some big furniture
that won't go through the doors.
It's putting them in the windows
of the top floor.
Why don't you take your donkey
up in the crane, and through the window?"

"All right," said Uncle Peppi.
"I will."

So Uncle Peppi and his grey donkey
went along with the people
who were moving on *that* day.

"What number is your flat?"
someone asked him.

"Ninety-six. It's on the top floor.
I'm taking my donkey up in the crane."

There was the crane
at the front of the block of flats
with ropes hanging down
in two big loops.

Uncle Peppi looped the ropes
round his grey donkey
and saw him lifted gently
up and up and up.

Then Uncle Peppi and some friends
went up quickly in the lift.
They went into Uncle Peppi's flat
and opened the big square windows
to help the grey donkey in.
He swung gently outside
just in the right place.

"Come along," said Uncle Peppi,
pulling gently at the donkey's collar,
but the donkey stuck out his four legs
and would not move.

"Come on. Come in the flat with me,"
said Uncle Peppi,
pulling harder.
But the donkey stuck out his four legs
and would not move.

"It's no good," said Uncle Peppi at
last. "We'll have to go back home."
So Uncle Peppi and his grey donkey
went back to their shabby little house
with the roof falling in
and the door falling off.

Next day a woman came
to Uncle Peppi, and said,

"Uncle Peppi, I have a flat
on the ground floor,
opening on to a little yard at the back.
Would you like me to change with you?"

"Oh, thank you," said Uncle Peppi.
"You are very kind."

"Well, let's go and see if your donkey
likes the idea," said the woman.
So Uncle Peppi and his grey donkey
went along to the block of flats
that rose like a tall white tower
into the blue sky.

They went to the ground floor flat,
and the woman opened the door for them.

"Come along," said Uncle Peppi,
pulling gently at his donkey's collar.
The donkey looked round for a moment.
Then he gave a soft little hee-haw
and trotted happily inside.

Small Poems

Lonely
A lonely bird
In a winter tree.
Not even a leaf
For company.

Little Boy
Without any shoes
In the field he goes,
And the dew-wet grass
Is washing his toes.

Mother Thrush to Baby Thrush
Open your mouth.
Open it wide,
And I'll pop a little worm inside.

Ragabones Rabbit

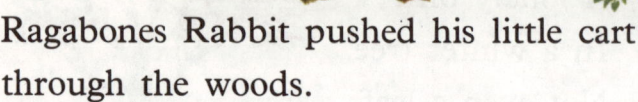

Ragabones Rabbit pushed his little cart through the woods.
"Rags and bones!" he shouted.
"Any rags and bones?"
He had a pile of rags and an old coat on his cart.
He also had a big bone
with quite a lot of meat on it,
and he had a jar
full of tiny paper windmills.

The windmills were red and blue
and yellow,
and each one was pinned to a stick.

"Windmills!" cried the field mice
and some of the birds
who came crowding round to look.

"Yes, windmills,"
said Ragabones Rabbit.
"I shall give a windmill to anyone
who brings me rags and bones today."

The first to bring something
was Robin, who had a bundle of feathers
from last year's nest.

"Here you are Ragabones Rabbit,"
she said.

"Thank you, thank you,"
said Ragabones Rabbit.
"Choose the windmill you would like."

Then along came Little Squirrel
with some old acorns.

"My mother says these are worn out,"
he said.

"Thank you, thank you,"
said Ragabones Rabbit.
"Choose the windmill you would like."

Then came Little Badger
with a roll of shabby straw.

"My mother says you may have
this old bedding," he said.

"Thank you, thank you,"
said Ragabones Rabbit.
"Choose the windmill you would like."
He put the feathers and the acorns
and the straw on his cart
and went on his way.

The animals went back through the trees
holding their little paper windmills.
The windmills blew round in the breeze
and made bright spots of red and blue
and yellow in the green woods.

Just then Little Hedgehog

came running up to Ragabones Rabbit.

"My mother hasn't anything to give you," she said. "She looked, but she couldn't find anything at all."

"Never mind," said Ragabones Rabbit, but he could see that Little Hedgehog wanted a windmill very much indeed. So he said,

"If you will help me to push the cart to the edge of the wood, I will give you a windmill."

"Oh, yes," replied Little Hedgehog and she helped to push the cart along the rough path.

In a little while
Ragabones Rabbit said,
"Just look after the cart for me
a moment. I have to get some things
from the foot of Owl's tree.
She'll be asleep, as you know,
and I don't want to wake her up
by taking the cart too near."

"All right," said Little Hedgehog,
and she stood by the cart
while Ragabones Rabbit
walked away through the trees.

Almost at once Little Hedgehog
heard footsteps. She looked up
and she saw Bad Fox coming.

"I have a bundle of things
for Ragabones Rabbit," said Bad Fox.
"I can't carry them
because I have a bad paw.
I've left them outside my den.
Will you run and get them for me please?"

Little Hedgehog did not know
whether she ought to go or not,

but she was glad to get away from Bad Fox
so she went.
Then Bad Fox jumped up on the cart
and hid himself under the old coat.

Little Hedgehog ran to Bad Fox's den,
but there was nothing outside it,
and when she came back to the cart
Bad Fox was not there.

"That's good," thought Little
Hedgehog. "He's gone."

Just then Ragabones Rabbit came back
with a bundle of things from Owl's tree,
and he and Little Hedgehog
went on pushing the cart
through the wood.

"It's very heavy," said Little
Hedgehog.

"Yes," said Ragabones Rabbit.
"I'm glad I have you to help me."

Soon they came to the edge of the wood.

"Thank you, Little Hedgehog,"
said Ragabones Rabbit.
"You must go back now,
but first you may choose
the windmill you would like."
Little Hedgehog took a yellow windmill
out of the jar.
Then she stood quite still.

She was frozen with fear,
for she saw something
sticking out from the old coat.
It was not a rag. It was not a bone.
It was a red-brown furry tail.

It was the tail of Bad Fox.

"Ragabones Rabbit," she whispered. "Did someone give you a furry tail to put on your cart?"

Ragabones Rabbit looked at the cart. Then *he* stood still,
frozen with fear, for he saw something sticking out from the old coat.
It was not a rag. It was not a bone.
It was a red-brown furry tail.
It was the tail of Bad Fox.

Then Ragabones Rabbit said in a loud voice,
"Little Hedgehog, please help me to push the cart
a little way along the road."
So Little Hedgehog helped to push the cart along the road.

Soon they came to the farm gate. Ragabones Rabbit stopped the cart and lifted off the jar of windmills.

"Hold those," he whispered to Little Hedgehog.

Then he gave a low whistle
to his friend the farm dog.
The dog came out at once.
He knew that Ragabones Rabbit
would have a bone for him.

"On the cart,"
whispered Ragabones Rabbit,
pointing to the red-brown furry tail
sticking out from the old coat.

The farm dog gave a loud "Woof!"
He jumped on the cart
and sent the rags and bones flying.
In a moment he was chasing Bad Fox
along the road.
Ragabones Rabbit laughed.

"I'll pick up the things,"
he said to Little Hedgehog.
"You run home now.
Thank you for helping me."

"Thank you. Goodbye, Ragabones
Rabbit," said Little Hedgehog,
and she turned back to the wood
with her yellow windmill
blowing round in the breeze.

Chick's Poem

Skies are high
   And seas are wide.
An egg is small
   To live inside.

Spider

A spider bought a bicycle.
He had it painted black.
He started off along the road
With an earwig on the back.
He sent the pedals round so fast,
He travelled all the day,
Then took the earwig off the back,
And put the bike away.

The Unkind Monkey

This is a story from Africa.

A tortoise and a monkey became friends.
One day the monkey gave a feast
and asked the tortoise to come to it.
He asked a number of monkeys as well,
and he set out a lot of good things
for them to eat.

The monkeys sat up to eat the food,
because they were made that way.
But the tortoise began to eat
with his four feet on the ground
because he was made *that* way.

" It is very bad manners to eat
while you are lying on the ground,"
said his monkey friend.
" You must sit up as we do."

So the tortoise tried to sit up,
but he kept falling down,
so that he had hardly any food at all.

He felt sad and angry, and he thought,
"The monkey is not a good friend.
He played a trick on me.
I will think of a trick to play on him."

A few days later
the tortoise gave a feast
and asked the monkey to come to it.
He asked a number of tortoises as well,
but he asked the tortoises to come
very early.

When they had arrived, he set fire
to a big patch of grass round his house
so that the monkey would have to walk
over black and burnt ground.
Then he set out a lot of good things
to eat.

Soon the monkey came along,
but by the time he reached
the tortoise's house
his paws were all dirty.

"It is very bad manners to eat
with dirty paws,"
said his tortoise friend.

"You had better go to the river
and wash them."

So the monkey went to the river
and washed his paws,
but when he came back he had to walk
over the black and burnt ground again.

"Your paws are still dirty,"
said his friend the tortoise crossly.

"You will have to go to the river
and wash them again."

So the monkey went to the river
and washed his hands a second time,
but of course, when he came back
he had to walk
over the black and burnt ground again.

"Your paws are *still* dirty,"
said his friend the tortoise,
and he made the monkey go back
to the river again,
and again
and again.

By that time the tortoises
had eaten all the good things
and there was nothing left
for the unkind monkey.

Adapted

A Page of Riddles

Q. What coat should be put on wet?
A. A coat of paint.

Q. Where does a rabbit keep its money?
A. In the bank.

Q. What time is it when an elephant sits on the fence?
A. Time to get a new fence.

Q. Why did the bus stop?
A. Because it saw a zebra crossing.

Q. What number gets bigger when it is turned over?
A. 6.

Treasure in the Well

Once upon a time
there were three brothers
who had a small farm of their own.
They lived in a white cottage
with a well at the side.
The well was full of clear fresh water
and it had never been known to run dry.

One very hot day in the spring
an old man went walking along the road
past the cottage.
He saw the three brothers
working on the farm, and he called out,
"I am very hot and thirsty.
Please may I have a drink
from your well?"

"Yes, of course,"
said the first brother,
and he went indoors to get a cup.
Then he turned the handle of the well
and pulled up the bucket
full of clear fresh water.

The old man drank gladly.
Then the second brother said to him,

"If you would like to rest
for an hour or two,
you could share our supper with us."

"Thank you," answered the old man.
" I will do that."

Then the third brother said,
" You may stay the night here if you wish. The barn is warm and dry, and there is soft hay to sleep on."

" Thank you," answered the old man.
" I will do that."
So the old man had supper
with the three brothers
and he slept all night in the barn.

When morning came,
the brothers gave him a loaf of bread
and another drink of water from the well.

" Now," said the old man,
"I must go on my way.
Thank you for all your kindness to me.
I wish I could repay you,
but I am very poor.
Besides, there is little you really need
while you have such a treasure
in your well."

The three brothers said goodbye

and watched the old man
walk up the road and out of sight.

As soon as he had gone,
they looked at each other and said,

"Treasure in our well?
What did he mean?"

"He must know something
that we don't know."

"Perhaps he threw a bag of money
down the well for us."

They wondered and wondered
what the treasure could be,
but as the well was full of water,
there was no way of finding out.

Now spring had come early
that year, and the days were very hot,
and there was no rain.

The ground became hard and dry
and the grass grew brown.

Then there was a long hot summer,
and still there was no rain.
The brothers had to use a lot of water
to keep the crops alive.

So the water in the well grew lower
and lower and lower,
and the little streams dried up,
and some of the crops faded
and the flowers died.
The hot weeks went on and on,
and still there was no rain.

Then one day the well ran dry.
The three brothers, of course,
were worried about the farm,
but they smiled and said to each other,

"Well, at least we'll be able
to go down the well
and see what the treasure is."

So the first brother tied a rope
round his waist,
and took a lantern in his hand.
The other two brothers let him down
slowly, slowly down the well.

Soon he reached the bottom
and stood on the muddy earth.
He held his lantern high.
He held his lantern low,

but all he found
was an old broken bucket.
Then he pulled the rope
to show the brothers
that he was ready to come up again.

"What did you find?" they asked,
as they helped him out of the well.

"Nothing but this old broken bucket,"
he said.

"I'll go down,"
said the second brother.

So he tied the rope round his waist,
and he took the lantern in his hand.
The other two brothers let him down
slowly, slowly down the well.

Soon he reached the bottom
and stood on the muddy earth.
He held his lantern high.
He held his lantern low,
but all he found was an old cracked cup.
Then he pulled the rope
to show his brothers
that he was ready to come up again.

"What did you find?" they asked,
as they helped him out of the well.

"Nothing but this old cracked cup,"
he said.

"*I'll* go down," said the third brother.
So he tied the rope round his waist,
and he took the lantern in his hand.
The other two brothers let him down
slowly, slowly down the well.

Soon he reached the bottom
and stood on the muddy earth.

He held his lantern high.
He held his lantern low,
but all he found was a little green frog.
Then he pulled the rope
to show his brothers
that he was ready to come up again.

" What did you find ? " they asked,
as they helped him out of the well.

" Nothing but this little green frog,"
he said.

" So there *isn't* any treasure,"
said the first brother,
" and now there isn't even any water.
I don't know *what* we are going to do
without it."

Then, just at that moment,
who should come along, but the old man !

" Good day. Good day," he said.

Then he pointed to the sky,
where a great black cloud
was drifting over the farm.

"Oh good, good!" cried the brothers.
"It's going to rain."
Even as they spoke it started to fall
in big, heavy, beautiful, wet drops,
feeding the thirsty plants,
beating on the cottage roof,
filling up the empty well.

That evening, as the three brothers
shared their supper with the old man,
they said,

"What did you mean last time you came?
You said there was a treasure in our
well. We have all been down to the
bottom and we have found nothing
except an old broken bucket,
and an old cracked cup
and a little green frog.
What treasure did you mean?"

"Why water of course!" said the old
man. "It's the greatest treasure on

earth, isn't it?"
The three brothers looked at the rain pouring down outside the window, and they smiled.

"I suppose it is," they said.

Funny Fish

Flatfish are flat,
And Flying Fish fly,
And Swordfish they look
    Like swords swimming by.

But Catfish don't purr,
And Dogfish don't bark,
And Starfish don't twinkle
    Down in the dark.

The Jumping Plate

No one will believe this story
because it is about a jumping plate.
It was a plain, white dinner plate
and it looked just the same
as all the other
plain, white dinner plates.
 There was only one thing different.
Underneath it there was a tiny dab
of blue paint.
Perhaps it *was* a tiny dab of blue paint
or perhaps it was a tiny dab of magic.
Who could tell?
 The plate was sent from a factory
to a shop. Then it was sent from the
shop to a school canteen,
with forty-nine other plates.
 The next day it was put on the table
in front of a boy called Derek
who stayed to school dinners.

Derek did not even know it was new,
and of course he did not know
it was a jumping plate.

On the jumping plate was Derek's
dinner—meat, potatoes, gravy and peas.
The dinner looked the same
as all the other dinners.
The plate looked the same
as all the other plates.

Derek began to eat,
and the plate began to jump.
At first it jumped only a little—
just enough to set the dinner trembling.
Then it jumped a little more,
enough to set the meat shivering
and shaking. Then it jumped a lot.

It set the meat shivering and shaking.
It set the potatoes dancing up and down.
It set the gravy spinning round
like a whirlpool,
and it set the peas hopping and jumping
over the table as if they were alive!

Some of the children looked shocked

because they thought Derek was naughty,
but some of them laughed
because they thought it was funny.

The lady who looked after the children
at dinner time was called Mrs North.
She did not think it was funny at all.

"What are you doing?" she asked
angrily.

"I can't help it," said Derek.
"It's the plate's fault. It's a jumping
plate."

"A jumping plate! How can it be?"
said Mrs North.
She cleared up the mess
and took the plate of food
back to the kitchen.
She emptied the food into a bin
and turned the plate upside down.

"Perhaps it's not flat," she thought.
But it *looked* flat.

"Nothing wrong with it," she thought,
but she did notice a tiny dab
of blue paint underneath.
Perhaps it *was* a tiny dab of blue paint
or perhaps it was a tiny dab of magic.
Who could tell?

The next day the jumping plate
was put on the table
in front of a little girl called Ann
who stayed to school dinners.
Ann did not even know it was new
and of course, she did not know
it was a jumping plate.

On the jumping plate was Ann's dinner

—fish, chips, tomato sauce and peas.
The dinner looked the same
as all the other dinners.
The plate looked the same
as all the other plates.

Ann began to eat,
and the plate began to jump.
At first it jumped only a little—
just enough to set the dinner trembling.
Then it jumped a little more—
enough to set the fish shivering
and shaking. Then it jumped a lot.

It set the fish shivering and shaking.
It set the chips dancing up and down.
It set the tomato sauce spinning round
like a whirlpool, and it set the peas
hopping and jumping over the table
as if they were alive!

Some of the children looked shocked
because they thought Ann was naughty,
but some of them laughed
because they thought it was funny.
Mrs North did not think it was funny

at all, but she felt very puzzled.

"What *are* you doing?" she asked in a surprised voice.

"I can't help it," said Ann unhappily. "It's the plate's fault. It's a jumping plate."

"A jumping plate!" said Mrs North. "How can it be?"

"It must be the one I had yesterday," said Derek.

"Yes, perhaps it is," said Mrs North. She cleared up the mess

and took the plate of food back
to the kitchen. Then she emptied it,
and looked underneath, thinking
that perhaps the plate was not flat.
It *looked* flat.

"Nothing wrong with it," she thought,
but she did notice a tiny dab
of blue paint underneath.
Perhaps it *was* a tiny dab of blue paint
or perhaps it was a tiny dab of magic.
Who could tell?

"Well anyway," thought Mrs North,
"it's the same plate that jumped about
yesterday. I'd better get rid of it."

She was just about to put it
in the rubbish bin, when Mrs Black,
who did the washing up, said,

"It seems a pity to throw away
a good plate. Let me have it.
I'll use it when we go camping
in the summer."

So Mrs Black washed and dried the plate
and took it home with her.

In the summer, the Black family
went on their camping holiday.
There were Mr and Mrs Black and Tommy
and Meg, and they put up their tent
in a big field near the sea.

On the first day the family sat down
to dinner. They sat on the grass
and used a box for a table.
Mrs Black warmed up some stew
she had brought from home.
It had meat and potatoes and gravy
and beans all mixed up together.
Mrs Black and the two children
had plastic picnic plates,
but Mr Black had a plain white plate.
It was, of course, the jumping plate,
and as soon as Mr Black began to eat,
the plate began to jump.

At first it jumped only a little—
just enough to set the dinner trembling.
Then it jumped a little more—
enough to set the meat shivering
and shaking. Then it jumped a lot.

It set the meat shivering and shaking.
It set the potatoes dancing up and down.
It set the gravy spinning round
like a whirlpool, and it set the beans
hopping and jumping over the table
as if they were alive!

Then Mrs Black remembered
that Mrs North had called it
a jumping plate.

"So it *is* a jumping plate," she said.
Quickly she fetched a plastic plate,
and put Mr Black's food on that.

Then after dinner,
she broke the jumping plate
into little bits and put them all
into the litter bin.
And that was the end of the
jumping plate.

The Blue Jackal

This is a story from India.
 There was once a jackal
who fell into a large pot of blue paint.
When he looked down at himself
and saw that he was blue
he crept away and hid in the jungle.
Then, after a while, he thought,
 "Why should I hide myself
just because I am blue?
Blue is a kingly colour.
I will pretend that I am a king."

So he went back to the other jackals
and walked proudly among them
with his head held high.
The other jackals did not know him.

"Who is this blue animal?" they asked.

"Blue is a kingly colour," answered
the blue jackal. "I am a king."

The other jackals did not know
he was just a jackal
so they began to obey his orders
and to act like servants to him.

Then, after a while,
the blue jackal thought,

"I am king of the jackals.
Why should I not be king
of the monkeys too?"
So he went to the monkeys
and walked proudly among them
with his head held high.
The monkeys did not know him.

"Who is this blue animal?" they asked.

"Blue is a kingly colour,"
replied the blue jackal.
"I am a king."

The monkeys did not know
he was just a jackal,
so they too, began to obey his orders
and to act like servants to him.

Then, after a while,
the blue jackal thought,

"I am king of the jackals
and king of the monkeys,
why should I not be king of the birds
and the snakes and the tigers

and the elephants?
Why should I not be king
of all the animals in the jungle?"

So the blue jackal made himself king
of the jackals and the monkeys
and the birds and the snakes
and the tigers and the elephants
and all the animals in the jungle.
They all obeyed his orders
and acted like servants to him.

He walked among them all
with his head held high,
and he became so proud
that he began to look down
on his own people, the jackals.

This made them very angry.

"I don't think he is a king at all,"
some of them said.

"I think he is really just a jackal
like ourselves."

Then a wise old jackal said,

"We will soon see if he is a jackal
or not.
This evening when I make a signal,
we will all give a great howl.
If he is really a jackal
like ourselves,
he will give a great howl in answer.
He will do it
before he has time to think."

So, that evening
when the wise old jackal made a signal,
all the other jackals gave a great howl.
It sounded loud and clear
in the still air.

The blue jackal lifted his head
and gave a great howl in answer.
He did it before he had time to think.

His howl sounded loud and clear
in the still air.

Then all the jackals knew
that he was not a king at all.
He was just a jackal
like themselves.

"He gave a howl like a jackal,"
they said.
"He is a jackal like ourselves."

Then the monkeys and the birds
and the snakes said,
"He gave a howl like a jackal.
He is not a king at all."

As for the tigers and the elephants,
they were so angry
that they chased the blue jackal
far, far into the jungle.
And there he stayed until the rains came
and washed all the blue paint away.
Then at last he looked
like the jackal that he really was.

Adapted

Up and Down

It's an up and down life,
It's an up and down life
For a baby kangaroo,
For he's whirled through the air
With every jump
That his mother wants to do.

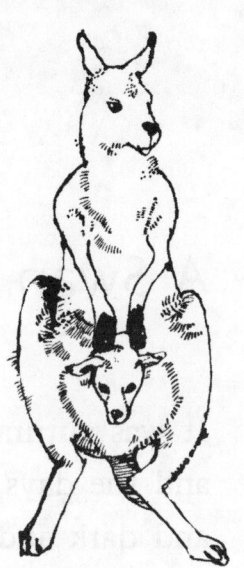

The Forest

I found a baby forest
  Of tiny little trees,
All straight and green and growing
  No higher than my knees.

A Swan for the Winter

It was autumn
and the days were getting cold
and dark and frosty.
Ingrid was looking out
for the wild swans.

Every year at this time,
they flew from Russia to England,
and on the way
they passed over Ingrid's house.
Ingrid's house was in Sweden
at the edge of a small lake.

Suddenly she saw them.

"Mother! Father!" she called.
"The wild swans are coming."

Mother and Father ran out of doors
and stood by the lake with Ingrid.

They all stared upwards.
The swans flew in a long line
across the clear, grey sky.
Their necks were stretched out
and their wings were beating.

"Aren't they beautiful?" said Mother.
Ingrid watched them
as they flew across the sky
into the distance, and out of sight.

"They've gone," she sighed.
Then suddenly she cried,
" Look! There's another one!
It's all by itself."
It was flying slowly, slowly,
far behind.

" It can't keep up with the others,"
said Father. " Poor thing!
There's something wrong with its wing."

At that moment
the swan seemed to give up hope.
It stopped flying.
One wing drooped to its side.
The big white body fell through the sky.
It fell, it fell, it fell with a splash
into the lake.

It fell over to one side
and flapped its good wing wildly,
so that the water was filled
with bubbles and foam.
Ingrid was nearly in tears.

"It will never catch up
with the other swans now," she said.

"Let's get some bread for it," said
Mother. She broke up some bread,
and Ingrid threw it into the water.
The swan was floating on the lake now,
and it pecked gladly at the food,
for it was very hungry.

Then, a little later
it walked on to the grassy bank
and sat under a small bush.

Father was good with birds and animals
and soon he tried to help the swan.
Mother had to hold its beak shut
while Father bound a strip of wood
to the broken wing.

At first the swan was angry and afraid
but suddenly it became quiet.

Perhaps it knew that Father and Mother
and Ingrid were trying to help it.

As the days went on, it learned
to trust them more and more.
Ingrid fed it every day,
and it began to follow her about.
It even followed her into the house,
walking round in a one-sided,
friendly way.

. . . . . .

Soon winter came.
Snow lay deep and white on the grass.
The waters of the lake froze
and turned to gleaming ice.
The swan was puzzled and unhappy.
This was just the sort of weather
it liked to leave behind in Russia.

"We'll have to let it indoors
at night," said Father,
so he and Ingrid
made a place for it to sleep
in the shed where the logs were kept.

Its wing seemed much better now
but it still walked in a one-sided way
and it followed Ingrid
nearly everywhere she went.

"How long do you think it will stay
with us?" she asked one day.

"All the winter for sure," said
Mother.

"Do you think it will stay
in the spring as well?" she asked.
Mother shook her head.

"No. When the spring comes
and the swans return,
I think it will want to fly
back to Russia with them."
Ingrid knew that Mother was right,
but she hoped and hoped
that the swan would stay.

. . . . .

Soon the days became warmer
and the snow began to melt.
The ice on the lake cracked
and floated away.
The swan ran round and round
on the grass, honking noisily
and flapping its wings.
It swam too, and beat up the water
into wide rings of bubbles and foam.

Then early one morning
while the moon was still shining
pale and cold,

Ingrid heard a great noise.
It came from the shed
where the swan slept.
It was honking loudly
and beating its wings against the door.

"Mother!" she called,
"there's something wrong with the swan."
But Mother was already awake,
and Father had run to the shed
to open the door.

Quickly Ingrid put on shoes
and a coat, and went out too.
The swan came rushing past her
like a great cloud of white.

Then it flapped its wings
and ran a little way
and rose into the air.

"It's flying!" said Ingrid.
"It's flying."

Then she looked up
and saw that the wild swans
were going back from England to Russia
as they did every year in the spring.

They flew in a long line
across the grey sky.

Their necks were stretched out
and their wings were beating.

Her own swan was flying up now.
It was just in time to join them.
Ingrid's eyes followed it
as it flew with them across the sky,
into the distance, and out of sight.

"It's gone," she sighed.
"Our swan has gone."

"People with people," said Father,
"and swans with swans.
That's the way of life, isn't it?"

Ingrid felt very sad,
but, for the swan's sake,
she felt very happy too.

Bricks and Mortar

Bricks and mortar,
Bricks and mortar,
Bricks and mortar
  Make a house.

Cheese and candles,
Cheese and candles,
Cheese and candles
  Feed a mouse.

Sand and pebbles,
Sand and pebbles,
Sand and pebbles
  Form a beach.

Stone and sweetness,
Stone and sweetness,
Stone and sweetness
   Fill a peach.

Winds and breezes,
Winds and breezes,
Winds and breezes
   Blow away.

Rain and sunshine,
Rain and sunshine,
Rain and sunshine
   Make our day.

The Canoe Race

Once upon a time
there were ten brothers.
They lived on a tiny island
in the wide Pacific Ocean.
Each of the brothers
wanted to be chief of the island,
so the eldest brother said,
 " We will have a canoe race
from here to the next island.
The boy who wins shall be chief."
 " Yes," agreed the others.
" That's a good idea."
 " But it's a very long way,"
said the youngest brother. "It will
take two or three days to get there."
 The boys put food and water
in their canoes,
and they put the paddles ready.
Then they all sat waiting

for the eldest brother to say " Go."

Just then their mother came
across the beach,
carrying a long bundle.

" I am coming with you," she said.
" Who will have me in his canoe ? "
No one answered.

" Well, who will have me ? "
she asked again. Still no one answered.
Then the eldest brother said,

" This is a race, Mother.
We can't take you.
You would make the canoe heavier
and the paddling harder."

The mother looked very hurt,
so the youngest brother said kindly,
"I will take you, Mother."
The mother smiled at him
and sat down in his canoe.
She put the long bundle at her feet.

"One, two, three, go!"
cried the eldest brother,
and the ten canoes started off
across the wide Pacific Ocean.

Even at the start of the race,
the youngest brother was left behind.
His canoe was heavier than the others,
and the paddling was harder.
All the same, he paddled and paddled
until night came.

The stars shone and his mother slept,
but the youngest brother
went on paddling all night long.

Next morning he could not see
the canoes of his nine brothers at all.
His mother awoke and sat up.
A little wind was blowing,

and she untied her long bundle.
"What is in that bundle?"
asked the youngest brother,
Then he saw a long pole and some ropes
and a roll of matting.
"No wonder the canoe is so heavy
and the paddling so hard," he said.
"Why did you bring these things?"

"You will see in a moment,"
said his mother.

She tied the mat to the long pole
and fixed it up in the canoe.
At once the wind filled the mat
and the canoe sped along.

"This is fine,"
said the youngest brother.
"I have never been so fast before.
But what will happen
if the wind blows the wrong way?"

Then his mother showed him
how to pull the ropes
so that they moved the mat
to catch the wind
if it blew the wrong way.

Soon the youngest brother
and his mother
were going so fast in their canoe
that they began to catch up
with the other brothers.

Soon they had passed them all,
except the eldest brother,
but later in the day
they caught up with him too.
He was very surprised to see them.

"What is that big thing in your canoe?"
he asked.

"Mother thought of it,"
replied the youngest brother.

"Give it to me," said the eldest
brother, and he paddled his canoe
close to the youngest brother's canoe.

The youngest brother tried
to drive him away with his paddle,
but his mother said,

"All right, we will change canoes."
So she and the youngest brother
stepped into the eldest brother's canoe,
and he stepped into theirs.
At once the wind filled the mat
and the eldest brother sped
across the wide Pacific Ocean.

"We should not have let him
have our canoe,"
said the youngest brother sadly.
Then he saw that his mother
had a roll of rope at her feet.

"I brought this with us," she said,
"so that your brother will not be able
to move the mat to catch the wind.
See! The wind is changing now
and he will soon find he is going
the wrong way. Now hurry!
We are very near the island.
Paddle as fast as you can

and you will still be first."

So the youngest brother paddled hard
and soon he reached the island.

"We are first after all," he said.
Then they pulled the canoe up
on the beach.
It was night again by then,
so they slept on the grass till morning.

All through the next day
the other brothers arrived.
They were very surprised to find
the youngest brother already there.
Each brother had to kneel to him
in turn, and say,

"You are our chief."

Last of all came the eldest brother

with the mat he could not use.
He had been blown far out of his way
and he was tired and very angry.
And the people of the tiny islands
in the wide Pacific Ocean say
that is the story of the very first sail.

Adapted from
"Fairy Tales from the Pacific Islands"
by A. W. Reed (Frederick Muller Ltd.)

Keys

Q. Which keys swing from trees?
A. Monkeys.

Q. Which keys have long ears?
A. Donkeys.

Q. Which keys make a gobbling noise?
A. Turkeys.

The Lost Key

One day the queen lost her key. She walked from the castle to the lake, but she did not find the key. She walked all round the lake, but she did not find the key. She walked back to the castle, and there was the key.

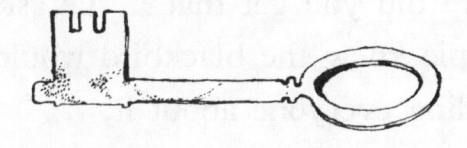

How the Blackbird Became Black

It is said that the blackbird
was once as white as snow.
He was a silly, lazy bird in those days.
He did not help his wife
to build a nest or feed the babies.
He just flew to and fro
chatting and fussing
about other birds' affairs.

One day he saw a magpie going into
a hollow tree.

"What have you got in there?"
asked the blackbird.

"Nothing much," said the magpie.
But the blackbird pushed his way in
and saw for himself.
He saw a pile of gold!

"Where did you get that?" he asked.
The magpie knew the blackbird would go
round telling everyone about it,

so he said.

"If I tell you, will you promise
not to tell anyone else?"

"I promise," said the blackbird.

"It was given to me
by the Dark Prince whose kingdom
is under the earth. I did some work
for him, and this was my payment."

"Oh," said the blackbird.
"Tell me how to get there, so that
I may go and offer to work
for him."

So the magpie took the blackbird
to a place in the wood
where there was a deep hole going down
into the earth.

"This is the entrance to the kingdom
of the Dark Prince," he said.
"It leads to a long passage.
If you go down it, you will pass
three rooms full of treasure.
The first room is filled with silver.
The second room is filled with jewels.
The third room is filled with gold.

Whatever you do, you must not touch
any of it. You will find the Dark Prince
at the end of the passage.
Ask him if you may work for him."

The blackbird was so eager
to get some treasure
that he hardly waited to say thank you
to the magpie.
He just flapped his wings and flew down
into the deep hole.

He flew along the passage
and soon he came to the first room.
It was filled with silver.
He longed to pick some up in his beak,
but he remembered

what the magpie had told him
and he did not touch it.

He flew on along the passage
and soon he came to the second room.
It was filled with jewels.
He longed to pick some up in his beak,
but he remembered
what the magpie had told him,
and he did not touch them.

He flew on along the passage
and soon he came to the third room.
It was filled with gold.
The walls were covered in gold.
The roof was covered in gold.
The floor was covered in gold.
There was gold everywhere.
It shone and sparkled and gleamed.

The greedy blackbird was so eager
to have some of it, that he forgot
what the magpie had told him.
He pushed his beak deep into the golden
dust that lay on the floor,
and picked up as much as he could.

At once there was a noise like thunder!
There was a great cloud of smoke.
There was a burst of leaping flames,
and there in the midst of them
was the Dark Prince!

The blackbird gave a scream.
He dropped his beakful of gold dust,
and he flew along the passage
and out into the fresh air above.

The blackbird is a much better bird
these days. He works hard.
He helps his wife to build the nest.
He helps to feed the babies.

He is, of course, no longer white.
He is black because his feathers were
burnt in the kingdom of the Dark Prince.
He is as black as black,
but his beak is bright yellow.
That is because it was covered

in gold dust, and he has never been able
to wash the colour off.

There is one other thing.
A blackbird will often fly
from the ground screaming,
as if it thinks the Dark Prince
may be just behind him.

Adapted

Dog Driver

He's climbing in the family car.
He's in the driver's seat.
His paws are on the steering wheel.
He's DRIVING down the street!
Oh dogs are not ALLOWED to drive,
As everybody knows,
But this one's SPEEDING through the town
And barking as he goes!

Bow-wow-wow, SMASH, SMASH!
Bow-wow-wow, CRASH, CRASH!

A Kangaroo Tale

There was once a man
who lived in a very big house
with a very big garden.
The garden had its own park and stream
as well as paths and lawns and flowers.

Long ago his grandfather had brought
two kangaroos over from Australia.
The two kangaroos had settled down
and had babies. The babies had grown up
and had babies themselves.
So the number of kangaroos
had become larger and larger
until now there were nearly twenty.

They lived freely and happily
in the parkland, running and jumping
and eating the fresh grass.

There was a high stone wall
all round the parkland.
Some of the bigger kangaroos

could have jumped over it
if they had wished to do so,
but they had plenty of food
so they never even thought of it.

Then one spring morning,
one kangaroo did jump over the wall.
He did not mean to do it.
He was just jumping very high
because it was springtime and he felt
strong and happy.
Then all of a sudden there he was
on the other side of the wall.

With another big jump he crossed
a road and landed in a field.
He went on jumping and jumping
until he was far away from his home.
He did not even guess
that he had jumped out of the parkland
and that he was really lost.

He did not guess that
until the middle of the morning,
when he found himself outside
a building on the edge of the village.

The building was a school.
The door was open,
and the kangaroo hopped inside.
He found himself in a cloakroom
where a lot of little coats were hanging
on rows of white pegs.
At one end were some washbasins
and two boxes of paper towels.
The kangaroo just stood and stared.

At that moment, inside a classroom,
a little girl called Judy
knocked over a pot of flowers.
She mopped up the water with a cloth.
Then she said to the teacher,

"Shall I go to the cloakroom
and give the flowers some more water?"

"Yes," said the teacher.
Judy took the pot of flowers
into the cloakroom.
She closed the door
of the classroom
and walked over to the washbasins.

Then she saw something

that nearly made her drop
the pot of flowers.
She saw a kangaroo!
She saw a large kangaroo,
standing still, staring at the basins.

Judy ran back like the wind.
In a second, she was inside
the classroom again,
with the door closed.
Her cheeks were pink, and her eyes
were wide and frightened.

"What's the matter, Judy?"
asked the teacher.

"There's something in the cloakroom,"
said Judy.

"What is it?" asked the teacher.
All the children were suddenly hushed
and still, waiting to hear the answer.

"It's a kangaroo," said Judy.

"A kanga-roo!" echoed a dozen voices.
The teacher laughed, and the children
laughed. Some of them laughed so much
that they nearly rolled
off their chairs.

Then at last when the room was nearly
quiet again, the teacher said
to one of the boys,

"Jeff, you give the flowers
some water, will you please?"

Jeff was very pleased. He took
the pot of flowers from Judy,
and he went out of the classroom.
He closed the door and walked over
to the washbasins.

Then he saw something
that nearly made him drop
the pot of flowers.
He saw a kangaroo!
He saw a large kangaroo, standing still,
staring at the basins!

Jeff ran back like the wind.
In a second, he was inside
the classroom again,
with the door closed.
His cheeks were pink, and his eyes
were wide and frightened.

"Well, Jeff?" asked the teacher.

"There *is* something in the cloakroom," said Jeff.

"What is it?" asked the teacher.

All the children were suddenly hushed
and still, waiting to hear the answer.
 " It's a kangaroo," said Jeff.
 " A kanga-roo! " echoed a dozen voices.
The teacher laughed and the children
laughed. Some of them laughed so much
that they nearly rolled
off their chairs.
 While they were laughing,
the kangaroo gave two jumps, and landed
back in the playground. One more jump
took him into the road,
and two more jumps took him
over the fields and far away.

 In the classroom the children
were still laughing.
Then the teacher said,
 " I think I'd better go and look."
She walked quietly into the cloakroom,
meaning the children to stay behind
in their chairs. But oh no,
the children could not do that!

They all went creeping after her.
If there was a kangaroo to be seen,
they wanted to see it!

The teacher walked
over to the washbasins.
She saw no kangaroo.
She saw nothing unusual at all.
The children all crept after her.
They saw no kangaroo.
They saw nothing unusual at all.

"Well Judy, where's your kangaroo?"
asked the teacher.

"It was there," said Judy.

"What do you say, Jeff?"
asked the teacher.

"He must have hopped away," said Jeff.

"Well, I think
you must have dreamed it,"
said the teacher,
and the children laughed and went back
to the classroom.

Two days later, the news was in the
newspaper. A kangaroo had been seen
in several different places.
It had been seen by a policeman
in one village,
and by a postman in another.
It had been seen by a lorry driver
along the road, and by a lady
near a town.

Everyone was talking about it,
and the children at school said,

"So Judy and Jeff must have seen

a kangaroo after all."

"Of course we saw it,"
said Judy and Jeff.

And what happened to the kangaroo?
Well, he spent four days jumping about.
Some people tried to catch him,
but he was much too quick for them.

Then at last, just by chance,
he came to his own part of the country
again. He came to the high stone wall
round the parkland.

Something seemed to tell him
that this was home. Perhaps he caught
the scent of his kangaroo friends
on the wind. Perhaps he knew the smell
of the wall, the trees, the grass.

Anyway, he gave a great jump
over the wall. This was his home,
and he was glad to be back.

Easter Egg

He made a golden Easter egg
That opened like a box,
With golden hinges at the side
And little golden locks.

He made a little silver chick,
With eyes of ruby red,
And tucked it in the Easter egg,
"A nice surprise!" he said.

Ragabones Rabbit and Little Owl

Ragabones Rabbit pushed his little cart
through the woods. He did not call out,
"Rags and bones," because he had
already been to the woods that week.
He looked up and saw Mrs Owl
in the tree above his head.
He knew that she usually slept
in the day time, so he said,
  "Hello Mrs Owl. Is anything wrong?"
  "Oh yes," replied Mrs Owl,
in a worried voice.

" Little Owl has flown away.
He must have gone while I was asleep.
You haven't seen him have you ? "

" No," said Ragabones Rabbit.

" Oh dear," went on Mrs Owl.
" I'm so afraid he will get lost or hurt.
He's much too small to be out alone."

" I'll keep a look out for him,"
said Ragabones Rabbit kindly,
" and if I find him,
I'll bring him straight back to you."

. . . . . .

Now Little Owl by this time,
had flown out of the wood
and along the road to the farm.
There he flew up to the roof
and sat on top of a chimney pot.

" What a long way I can see from here,"
he said to himself. " I can see— "
But oh ! Little Owl leaned over
a little too far,
and in a moment he had fallen

down the chimney
into the sooty darkness.

That afternoon the farmer's wife
was sitting mending socks.
It was a fine spring day
so there was no fire in the room
but suddenly a lump of soot
fell down into the grate
and over the rug.
The farmer's wife jumped to her feet.
Then there was a flop, flop, flop,
and down came some more soot.
It fell on the rug and the carpet.

"Oh dear! What a mess!"
sighed the farmer's wife.
"I hope that's all for now."
But it was not all, not quite.

There was a flop, flop, flop,
and one more rather heavy flop,
and down came
a fat little sooty black ball.
It looked for all the world
like a bundle of rags.

It was, as you can guess, Little Owl.

He was too frightened to move.
He could not see
because his eyes were full of soot.
He could not hear
because his ears were full of soot.
He could not cry out
because his mouth was full of soot.

He did not know where he was
or what had happened to him.
He stayed quite still
where he had fallen.

"However did that bundle of rags

fall down our chimney?"
thought the farmer's wife.
She swept up the soot
and put it in a pile on the grass
at the back of the barn.
She knew that soot was good
to use on the garden.

She swept up
the still, silent Little Owl
and put him on the grass
beside the pile of soot.

The farm dog came fussing up
to the farmer's wife.
He sniffed at the still, silent
Little Owl and did a dog dance
round him. He sniffed and smelled
and barked at him.

"Silly old dog," said the farmer's
wife. "It's only a bundle of rags,
though how it fell down our chimney
I shall never know."
Then she went indoors to clean the rug
and the carpet.

Little Owl was still too frightened
to move. He could not see
because his eyes were full of soot.
He could not hear
because his ears were full of soot.
He could not cry out
because his mouth was full of soot.
He still did not know where he was
or what had happened to him.

Just then the farm dog heard
Ragabones Rabbit's voice from the road,

"Rags and bones! Any rags and bones?"
The farm dog ran through the gate.

"Ragabones Rabbit," he said,
"There's a small bundle of rags
at the back of the barn.
Would you like to come and see it?"

"Yes please," replied Ragabones Rabbit
and he walked with the farm dog
to the back of the barn.

"There," said the farm dog,
waving a paw at the little black bundle
on the grass.

"Mm," began Ragabones Rabbit slowly.
"It's a bit too dirty for me, I'm afraid.
Seems to be all sooty."

"Yes," agreed the farm dog.
"It is a bit sooty.
Fell down our chimney it did."

"I won't take it if you don't mind,"
said Ragabones Rabbit.
"Thanks all the same."
He stared at the little black bundle.
It seemed to remind him of something,
but he did not know what.

Then at that very moment
the little black bundle opened
its sooty beak and gave
a sad and frightened little hoot.

The farm dog nearly jumped
out of his skin.
"It spoke!" he barked.
"I seem to know that voice,"
said Ragabones Rabbit,
"but I can't think . . ."
He picked up the little black bundle
in his paws and gave it a little shake.
Some of the soot fell off.
He shook it again. Now he could see
brown feathers showing through.
"Are you Little Owl?" he asked.
"Yes," choked Little Owl.
"Well!" said the farm dog.
Ragabones Rabbit washed Little Owl
under the farmyard tap,
and dried him with a rag from his cart.
"Now I'll take you back
to your mother," he said.
He lifted Little Owl on to his cart
and pushed the cart all the way
back to the woods.
Mrs Owl came flying down at once.

"Mrs Owl," said Ragabones Rabbit,
"there's something on my cart for you."
He pulled aside a bit of pink cloth,
and there, on a nest of rags
was Little Owl.
He was still a little ruffled
and damp and dirty,
and he was fast asleep.

Snow

Softly the snow came down at night
And covered all the world with white.
I thought I'd be the first to go
And leave my footprints in the snow,
But there beyond the gate I found
A small dog's pawprints on the ground,
And little birds *their* marks had spread
   While I had been asleep in bed.

The Christmas Tree

Gleaming tinsel, balls of glass,
    And bells of frosty white,
These are all the things we'll put
    Upon our tree tonight.

Stars of silver, stars of gold,
    And birds with glist'ning wings,
Paper lanterns red and blue,
    And little shining things.

Coloured snowflakes, crackers gay,
    So bright and fair to see.
These are all the things we'll put
    Upon our Christmas tree.

The Red Sledge

Rudl was a boy
who lived in Switzerland.
He lived in a house made of wood
and stone. It was built high
on the side of a mountain,
where the snow lay deep all the winter.

He had no brothers or sisters
but he spent hours and hours playing
in the snow with his sledge and his dog.

The sledge was painted bright red,
and there were lots of gentle slopes
near the house, where he could use it.
He would sit on the sledge
with his feet up in front of him.
He would hold on tightly
and he would whizz down like the wind.

Rudl's dog was a very big one
rather like a wolf. He was called Pax.
He was very strong but very gentle.

When Rudl whizzed down the slopes
on his sledge, Pax would run along
behind him, sending the snow flying
in a cloud of white.

One morning Father said to Rudl,

"I'm going to see Grandfather today.
Would you like to come with me?"

"Yes please," said Rudl.
Grandfather lived
lower down the mountain.

Rudl and his father set off
with Pax barking beside them.
Rudl pulled his red sledge along,
and sometimes when there was a slope
that was not too steep, he would sit
on the sledge and go whizzing down.
Then he would wait for his father
to catch up with him.

For a while all went well.
Then something happened.
Rudl was sledging down a gentle slope,
when suddenly he skidded,
and the sledge went shooting off
the wrong way. Rudl tried to turn it,
but the snow was very slippery
in that place and he could not do much
to help himself.

The sledge went rushing onwards
like the wind. It went rushing onwards
towards a rocky place
where the mountain dropped down steeply
like the edge of a cliff.
If Rudl could not stop

before he reached that place,
he would tumble down and down and down.

Father knew this, and he ran after him,
but he could not go
as fast as the sledge.
Pax knew it too and he ran like the wind.
Could he catch up the sledge?
Could he? Could he? Yes, he could.
He threw his great furry body at Rudl
and tried to knock him off in the snow
before it was too late.

"Let go. Let go," he tried to say,
but Rudl was too frightened
to do anything but cling on tightly.

Pax tried again.
With another rush, he caught up
with the sledge again.
With a great jump he threw
his great furry body at Rudl
and tried to knock him off into the snow
before it was too late.

"Let go. Let go," he tried to say,
but Rudl was still too frightened

to do anything but cling on tightly.

In a moment it *would* be too late.
In a moment Rudl and the sledge
would reach the rocky place
where the mountain dropped down steeply
like the edge of a cliff.
In a moment, Rudl and the sledge
would tumble down and down and down.

Pax tried again, and he knew
that this would be the last chance.
With a mighty jump
like the jump of a wild wolf,
he threw his great furry body at Rudl.
The sledge trembled a moment.
Rudl over-balanced a little.
He put out his hands to save himself.

Next moment he had fallen
off the sledge into the soft snow
with Pax on top of him,
and the red sledge was tumbling
over and over, down and down and down.

A little later, Father and Rudl
and Pax were all together again.

Rudl was half crying and half laughing, and saying,

"Pax was a bad dog to push me off the sledge."

But Father was hugging Rudl and Pax in turn, and saying,

"Pax was a good dog, a clever dog, a wonderful dog!
He saved your life, Rudl."

And what happened to the sledge?
Well, far down below, Grandfather
was digging some of the snow away
from his front door.
The sun was shining
and all the fir trees were gleaming
and sparkling.

"It's a lovely day,"
thought Grandfather,
and he looked up at the blue sky.
Suddenly he saw something—
something bright red.

For a moment he thought it was falling
from the sky, but then he knew
it must be tumbling down
from higher up the mountain.
What was it?
Whatever could it be?
Then it landed among the trees
a little distance away.

Grandfather dropped his spade and
hurried to the spot. He saw
that a branch had been broken off

one of the smaller trees.
He saw that on the snow beside it
was a bright red sledge.

Grandfather was filled with fear.
He knew only one person
who had a bright red sledge,
and that was his grandchild, Rudl.
It was Rudl's sledge. It must be.
But where was Rudl?
He must be lying somewhere
on the mountain, badly hurt.

Grandfather had never felt
so frightened in his life.
He held his hands round his mouth,
and gave a long, loud call.

The call sounded right up the mountain
to Rudl and Father and Pax.

"It's Grandfather," said Rudl.
Then Father held his hands round
his mouth,
and gave a long, loud call, which meant,
"It's all right."
And Pax gave a great, loud bark,
as if he too were trying to say,
"Yes. It's all right."

Small Stories

1

Long ago an artist painted a picture
of a boy with a bowl of grapes
in his hand.
The grapes looked so real
that some birds flew onto the picture
and pecked at them.
This made the artist cross.

" If I had made the boy look as real
as the grapes," he said,
" the birds would not have dared to
touch them."

2

In the time of King Charles II
an artist painted a full-length picture
of his own wife.
To his horror, his wife's pet dog
jumped up and scratched the picture
again and again. He was trying
to get up into the lady's lap.

A Nonsense Tale

There was once a gypsy man
who lived in a caravan
with his wife and his dog.
 Early one morning
he was walking across a field
when he fell into a hole.
It had once been the entrance
to an old mine
but it had not been used for many years.
 He felt himself falling down, down, down
until at last he reached the bottom.
Luckily he was not hurt,
and when he had rested a little,
he thought,
 " Now I'm down here
I might as well look round."
 It was very dark,
but he felt his way along a passage.
Slowly it became lighter

until he could see quite clearly.

"It's very strange down here,"
he thought, and the further he walked,
the stranger it became.
These were some of the things he saw.

He saw a farmer ploughing a lake.
He was leading four horses.
The four horses were pulling the plough
across the calm blue water.

He saw a green field
with a ship sailing on it.

He saw a donkey
riding on the back of a man.

He saw a road mender
breaking up stones with a feather.
He saw a woman carrying water
in a sieve.
This made him feel thirsty
and hungry too.
The woman was walking in the garden
of her cottage,
so the gypsy went up to her and said,
"I am very hungry.
Please can you give me something to eat?"
"Yes, of course," she answered.
"Come into the garden
and take some puddings
from the pudding tree."
The gypsy went into the garden
and there he saw a tree
with puddings hanging from every branch.
He ate all he needed
and he had a drink of water
from the sieve.
Then he said thank you to the woman
and went on along the road.

Soon he met some gypsies.
He was pleased to see
some of his own people,
though they were not quite like
the gypsies above ground.

"Where are you going?" he asked them.

"We are going across the sea,"
they answered. "Come with us.
Look! There is our ship."

"Thank you," said the man.
"I will gladly come with you."

So he stepped into the ship with them
and began to sail across the sea.

As the hours went by,
the gypsies became hungry.

"We'll make a camp fire,
and cook a meal," they said.
So they stepped out of the ship
and lit a fire upon the sea.
They cooked a fine meal
and sat by the fire to eat it.

Then they went back into the ship
and sailed on again.

At last, just before sunset,
the ship came to land on a quiet beach.

"Goodbye," said the gypsies,
and in a moment they had all gone,
and the man was left alone.
But no! He was not quite alone,
for there was his own caravan,
and there were his wife and his dog
waiting for him.

The gypsy man
never went underground again.
In fact he never even found the hole
he had fallen down.

Adapted from
"The Yellow Dragon and Other Gypsy Folk Tales"
by John Hampden (Andre Deutsch Ltd., 1969)

Helpful Teddy

Little children who are deaf find it very hard to learn to talk. They cannot hear other people speak, and they cannot tell if the sounds they make are right.

Some hospitals and schools for deaf children have thought of a clever way of helping them. They have a big fluffy teddy bear. He looks like any other teddy bear, but he has a tiny machine in his head or his chest.

If a child sits in front of him and tries to talk, Teddy's machine picks up the sound. Then lights glow in his eyes. If the child makes the sounds well, Teddy's eyes become brighter. If the sound is not so good, his eyes become dimmer.

The children love him and he is a great help to them.